P9-DND-612

SUPER SANDCASTLE
Super Simple Cooking

Super Simple
Holiday Treats

Easy No-Bake Recipes for Kids

Nancy Tuminelly

Consulting Editor, Diane Craig, M.A./Reading Specialist

ABDO
Publishing Company

Published by ABDO Publishing Company, 8000 West 78th Street, Edina, Minnesota
55439. Copyright © 2011 by Abdo Consulting Group, Inc. International copyrights
reserved in all countries. No part of this book may be reproduced in any form without
written permission from the publisher. Super SandCastle™ is a trademark and logo of
ABDO Publishing Company.

Printed in the United States of America, North Mankato, Minnesota
052010
092010

 PRINTED ON RECYCLED PAPER

Editor: Katherine Hengel
Content Developer: Nancy Tuminelly
Cover and Interior Design and Production: Colleen Dolphin, Mighty Media
Photo Credits: Colleen Dolphin, iStockphoto (Tammy Bryngelson, Dawna Stafford),
Shutterstock
Food Production: Colleen Dolphin, Kelly Dolphin

The following manufacturers/names appearing in this book are trademarks:
Target® Plastic Wrap, Pyrex® Measuring Cup, Reynolds® Cut-Rite® Wax Paper,
Pam® Cooking Spray

Library of Congress Cataloging-in-Publication Data

Tuminelly, Nancy, 1952-
   Super simple holiday treats : easy no-bake recipes for kids / Nancy Tuminelly.
     p. cm. -- (Super simple cooking)
   ISBN 978-1-61613-386-3
   1. Holiday cookery--Juvenile literature. 2. Quick and easy cookery--Juvenile literature.
I. Title.
   TX739.2.C45T96 2011
   641.5'68--dc22
                              2009053189

Super SandCastle™ books are created by a team of professional educators, reading
specialists, and content developers around five essential components—phonemic
awareness, phonics, vocabulary, text comprehension, and fluency—to assist young
readers as they develop reading skills and strategies and increase their general
knowledge. All books are written, reviewed, and leveled for guided reading, early
reading intervention, and Accelerated Reader® programs for use in shared, guided,
and independent reading and writing activities to support a balanced approach to
literacy instruction.

Note to Adult Helpers

Helping kids learn how to cook is fun!
It is a great way for them to practice
math and science. Cooking teaches kids
about responsibility and boosts their
confidence. Plus, they learn how to help
out in the kitchen! The recipes in this
book require very little adult assistance.
But make sure there is always an adult
around when kids are in the kitchen.
Expect kids to make a mess, but
also expect them to clean up after
themselves. Most importantly, make
the experience pleasurable by sharing
and enjoying the food kids make.

Symbols

 knife
Always ask an adult to help
you cut with knives.

 microwave
Be careful with hot food!
Learn more on page 5.

 nuts
Some people can get very
sick if they eat nuts.

Contents

Let's Cook!

The recipes in this book are simple! You don't even need an oven or stove! Cooking teaches you about food, measuring, and following directions. It's fun to make good food! Enjoy your tasty creations with family and friends!

Bon appétit!

Cooking Basics

Before You Start...

- Get permission from an adult.
- Wash your hands.
- Read the recipe at least once.
- Set out all the ingredients, tools, and equipment you will need.
- Keep a towel close by for cleaning up spills.

When You're Done...

- Cover food with plastic wrap or **aluminum** foil. Use containers with tops when you can.
- Put all the ingredients and tools back where you found them.
- Wash all the dishes and **utensils**.
- Clean up your work space.

4

Using the Microwave

- Use dishes that are microwave-safe.

- Never use **aluminum** foil or metal.

- Start with a short cook time. If you need to, add a little more.

- Use oven mitts when removing something.

- Stir liquids before and during heating.

How to Melt Chocolate in the Microwave

Microwave the chocolate for 30 seconds. Using oven mitts, take it out and stir. Repeat until most of the chocolate is melted. Then you can stir until it is smooth. Be patient! If you overcook the chocolate, you have to start over!

Measuring Tips

Wet Ingredients
Set a measuring cup on the countertop. Add the liquid until it reaches the amount you need. Check the measurement from eye level.

Dry Ingredients
Dip the measuring cup or spoon into the dry ingredient. Scoop out a little more than you need. Use the back of a dinner knife to scrape off the **excess**.

Moist Ingredients
Ingredients like brown sugar and dried fruit are a little different. They need to be packed down into the measuring cup. Keep packing until the ingredient reaches your measurement line.

Do You Know This = That?

There are different ways to measure the same amount.

3 teaspoons = 1 tablespoon

4 tablespoons = ¼ cup

5 tablespoons + 1 teaspoon = ⅓ cup

16 tablespoons = 1 cup

1 cup = 8 ounces

1 stick of butter = ½ cup

2 cups = 1 pint

4 cups = 1 quart

2 quarts = ½ gallon

Cooking Terms

Beat

Stir with a spoon, whisk, or beaters until smooth.

Grease

Coat the inside of a pan with butter, oil, or spray.

Mash

Crush food until soft with fork or masher.

Melt

Heat something solid until it is **softened**.

Mix

Combine ingredients with a mixing spoon.

Scrape

Run the edge of a spatula along the sides of a bowl.

Slice

Cut into thin pieces with a knife.

Spread

Make a smooth layer with a spoon, knife, or spatula.

Keeping Food Fresh

Storing Food

Use **airtight** containers. They have tight lids to keep air out. Plastic zip top bags are good airtight containers too.

Covering Food

Use plastic wrap to cover food going in the refrigerator or on the countertop. Be careful not to put the plastic wrap on too tight. It can stick to your topping!

Tools

Here are some of the tools that you'll need to get started.

9 x 13-inch baking dish

cutting board

baking sheet

microwave-safe mixing bowls

pitcher

tall sundae glasses

measuring cups
(dry ingredients)

measuring cup
(wet ingredients)

measuring spoons

silicone spatula

mixing spoon

plastic wrap

large spoon

wax paper

can opener

oven mitts

sharp knife

heart-shaped
cookie cutter

dinner knife

whisk

ice cream scoop

toothpicks

Ingredients

Fresh Produce

- oranges
- strawberries
- blueberries
- snap peas
- baby carrots
- celery sticks
- grape tomatoes

Frozen

- whipped topping
- vanilla ice cream

Other

- dry-roasted peanuts
- vanilla wafer cookies
- peanut butter
- crispy rice cereal
- matzo crackers
- grape juice
- orange juice
- lemon-lime soda
- maraschino cherries
- corn flake cereal
- assorted dried fruits (figs, papaya, dates)
- medium whole-wheat tortillas
- honey graham cereal squares

Dairy

- [ ] butter
- [ ] egg yolks
- [ ] blueberry yogurt
- [ ] ranch dip

Baking Aisle

- [ ] cooking spray
- [ ] light corn syrup
- [ ] sugar
- [ ] Chinese five-spice powder
- [ ] baking soda
- [ ] white chocolate chips
- [ ] green food coloring
- [ ] green gumdrops
- [ ] green decorating sugar
- [ ] red, pink, and green icing
- [ ] semisweet chocolate chips

- [ ] peppermint extract
- [ ] dark-chocolate almond bark
- [ ] cocoa powder
- [ ] cinnamon
- [ ] ground ginger
- [ ] nutmeg
- [ ] 9-inch graham cracker piecrust
- [ ] small red and green spice drops
- [ ] miniature marshmallows
- [ ] vanilla extract
- [ ] canned pumpkin
- [ ] cocoa
- [ ] honey

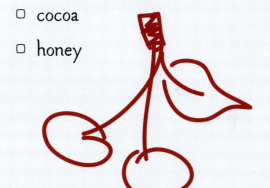

Chinese New Year Munch

Crunch your way into the year!

Makes 20 servings

Ingredients

cooking spray

½ cup light corn syrup

1 cup sugar

2 cups dry roasted peanuts

¾ teaspoon Chinese five-spice powder

1 teaspoon butter

1 teaspoon baking soda

Tools

• baking sheet

• measuring cups

• measuring spoons

• large, microwave-safe bowl

• mixing spoons

• oven mitts

• silicone spatula

• wax paper

14

1 Grease baking sheet lightly with cooking spray.

2 Mix corn syrup, sugar, peanuts, and five-spice powder together in large microwave-safe bowl.

3 Microwave on high for 2 minutes and stir. Continue to microwave and stir until melted. Mix in butter with spoon. Microwave for 30 seconds and stir until smooth.

4 Mix in baking soda until foamy.

5 Grease spatula with spray. Take mixture out of bowl and place on baking sheet. Put wax paper on top. Be careful! It's still very hot. Use back of spoon to press into thin layer. Cover and cool at least 1 hour.

6 Break into pieces. Eat or store!

Valentine Crispies

Eat your heart out!

Makes 8 cookies

Ingredients

1 cup semisweet chocolate chips

¼ cup light corn syrup

2 tablespoons butter

½ teaspoon peppermint extract

3 cups crispy rice cereal

pink and red icing

small candy hearts

Tools

• baking sheet

• wax paper

• measuring cups

• measuring spoons

• large, microwave-safe bowl

• oven mitts

• mixing spoon

• spatula

• heart-shaped cookie cutter

1 Cover baking sheet with wax paper.

2 Combine chocolate chips, corn syrup, and butter together in large microwave-safe bowl. Stir with mixing spoon. Microwave on high for 1 minute and stir with spoon. Continue to microwave for 20 seconds at a time. Stir until melted.

3 Stir in peppermint with mixing spoon. Mix in cereal gently until evenly covered with chocolate mixture.

4 Quickly spread cereal mixture on baking sheet with spatula. Put wax paper on top and press mixture down with your hands. Cover and **chill** for 20 minutes until slightly firm.

5 Carefully cut into hearts with cookie cutter. **Decorate** with icing and candy hearts. Cover and chill until firm. Eat or store!

Leprechaun Lollipops

May these treats bring you luck!

Makes 10 cookies

Ingredients

20 vanilla wafer cookies

½ cup peanut butter

12-ounce bag white chocolate chips

green food coloring

green gumdrops

green icing

green decorating sugar

Tools

- dinner knife
- 10 craft sticks
- 2 medium microwave-safe bowls
- oven mitts
- mixing spoon
- wax paper

1. Spread peanut butter on flat sides of ten cookies. Put craft stick in middle of each cookie. Top with another cookie to make a sandwich around the stick.

2. Divide chips into two medium microwave-safe bowls. Microwave each on high for 30 seconds. Stir with mixing spoon. Repeat until melted.

3. Add several drops of food coloring to one bowl of melted chips. Stir to make green chocolate.

4. Dip lollipops in either white or green chocolate. Cover cookies completely.

5. Lay on wax paper. **Chill** at least 30 minutes.

6. **Decorate** using green gumdrops, icing, and decorating sugar.

Mazel Tov Matzo Cakes

Celebrate with a chocolate surprise!

Makes 8 servings

Ingredients

5 ounces dark-chocolate almond bark

2 tablespoons cocoa powder

12 tablespoons butter (1½ sticks)

2 egg yolks

½ cup sugar

2 tablespoons cocoa

4 large matzo crackers

Tools

- 2 microwave-safe bowls
- oven mitts
- measuring cups
- measuring spoons
- mixing spoons
- whisk
- silicone spatula

1. Combine chocolate and cocoa powder in microwave-safe bowl. Microwave for 30 seconds and stir. Let cool.

2. Put butter in another microwave-safe bowl. Microwave on high for 30 seconds then stir. Repeat until melted.

3. Add yolks to butter. Whisk until smooth. Add sugar slowly and continue to beat until mixed well.

4. Scrape chocolate mixture into butter mixture. Beat with whisk to make a smooth spread.

5. Spread chocolate over two matzo crackers with spatula. Put remaining crackers on top of the chocolate. Spread another layer of chocolate on top. Cover and **chill** for at least 1 hour. Cut each cake into four pieces.

Cinco de Mayo Fizzies

A bubbly drink for a Mexican fiesta!

Makes 4 glasses

Ingredients

1 cup grape juice

1 cup orange juice

1½ cups lemon-lime soda

ice cubes

8 maraschino cherries

1 slice of fresh orange

Tools

• measuring cups

• pitcher

• mixing spoon

• drinking glasses

• knife

• cutting board

1. Pour grape juice, orange juice, and soda into pitcher. Stir gently with spoon. Add more soda if you like more fizz.

2. Fill glasses with ice. Pour juice mixture into each glass.

3. Cut orange slice into four pieces. **Garnish** each glass with two cherries and one orange piece.

If you want, you can double this recipe! Muy bien!

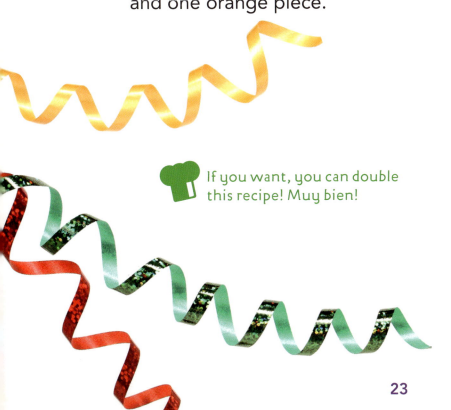

Red, White & Blue Trifle

Celebrate the 4th of July with this dessert!

Makes 1 serving

Ingredients

6 ounces blueberry yogurt

½ cup fresh strawberries, sliced

1 cup whipped topping, thawed

½ cup corn flake cereal

¼ cup fresh blueberries, rinsed

Tools

• large sundae glass
• spoon
• knife
• cutting board
• measuring cups

1. Spoon blueberry yogurt into large sundae glass.

2. Slice strawberries with knife. **Arrange** strawberries over yogurt.

3. Spoon half of the whipped topping over strawberries. Smooth with spoon.

4. Sprinkle cereal over whipped topping. Spoon other half of whipped topping over cereal and smooth with spoon.

5. **Garnish** with sliced strawberries and fresh blueberries. Eat immediately!

Rinse fresh strawberries and blueberries under running water. Put in strainer to **drain**.

Halloween Pumpkin Pie

A Halloween delight for all!

Makes 8 servings

Ingredients

9-inch graham cracker pie crust

1 quart vanilla ice cream

⅓ cup sugar

1 teaspoon cinnamon

½ teaspoon ground ginger

¼ teaspoon nutmeg

1 cup canned pumpkin

assorted dried fruits (figs, papaya, dates)

Tools

- ice cream scoop
- large mixing bowl
- can opener
- mixing spoon
- medium bowl
- measuring cups
- measuring spoons
- knife
- cutting board
- plastic wrap

1. Let ice cream sit out for 15 minutes. Scoop ice cream into large bowl. Mash with fork.

2. Stir sugar, cinnamon, ginger, nutmeg, and canned pumpkin together in medium bowl. Add to ice cream and stir together until well mixed.

3. Spoon mixture into pie crust and smooth top. Cover with plastic wrap. Freeze for at least 2 hours.

4. Before serving, **decorate** pie with dried fruit. Cut out triangles for the eyes. Use a dried date for the nose. Cut squares for teeth.

5. Let pie sit out for 5 minutes. Slice with knife and serve.

Horn of Veggies

Healthy Thanksgiving treats!

Makes 4 servings

2 medium whole-wheat tortillas

snap peas

baby carrots

celery sticks

grape tomatoes

ranch dip

Tools
• sharp knife

• cutting board

• toothpicks

28

1. Cut each tortilla in half with knife.

2. Roll each half into cone with rounded edge at open end. Use toothpicks to hold cone shape.

3. Fill each cone with snap peas, carrots, celery, and grape tomatoes.

4. Serve with ranch dip!

Try adding baby corn!

Christmas Gumdrop Bars

A delicious dessert for Santa's helpers!

Makes 36 bars

Ingredients

cooking spray

13-ounce package honey graham cereal squares

2 cups small red and green spice drops

1½ cups white chocolate chips

10-ounce package miniature marshmallows

⅓ cup butter

¼ cup honey

1 teaspoon ground ginger

1 teaspoon vanilla extract

Tools

- large microwave-safe bowls
- measuring cups
- mixing spoons
- oven mitts
- measuring spoons
- 9 x 13-inch baking dish
- wax paper
- knife

1. Grease large bowl with cooking spray. Mix cereal and spice drops together in bowl.

2. In another large bowl, microwave chips for 30 seconds and then stir. Repeat until melted. Stir in marshmallows. Microwave on high for 30 seconds. Stir and repeat until marshmallows are melted.

3. Add butter and honey to marshmallow mixture. Microwave for 30 seconds and stir until smooth. Mix ground ginger and vanilla. Pour marshmallow mixture over cereal mixture. Mix gently with spoon.

4. Grease baking dish. Put marshmallow and cereal mixture in dish. Place wax paper on top and press evenly. Let cool for 30 minutes. Cut into 36 bars.

Glossary

aluminum – a light metal.

arrange – to place in a certain order or pattern.

chill – to put something in the refrigerator to make it cold or firm.

coat – to cover with a thin layer.

decorate – to add items to make something look different or more fancy.

drain – to remove liquid using a strainer.

excess – more than the amount wanted or needed.

garnish – to decorate with small amounts of food.

soften – to bring to room temperature or make less firm.

sturdy – strong and well built.

utensil – a tool used to prepare or eat food.

About SUPER SANDCASTLE™

Bigger Books for Emerging Readers Grades K–4

Created for library, classroom, and at-home use, Super SandCastle™ books support and engage young readers as they develop and build literacy skills and will increase their general knowledge about the world around them. Super SandCastle™ books are an extension of SandCastle™, the leading preK–3 imprint for emerging and beginning readers. Super SandCastle™ features a larger trim size for more reading fun.

Let Us Know

Super SandCastle™ would like to hear your stories about reading this book. What was your favorite page? Was there something hard that you needed help with? Share the ups and downs of learning to read. We want to hear from you! Send us an e-mail.

sandcastle@abdopublishing.com

Contact us for a complete list of SandCastle™, Super SandCastle™, and other nonfiction and fiction titles from ABDO Publishing Company.

www.abdopublishing.com
8000 West 78th Street, Edina, MN 55439
800-800-1312
952-831-1632 fax